THE TEACHING OF READING: WHAT TEACHERS NEED TO KNOW

UNITED KINGDOM READING ASSOCIATION

The Teaching of Reading: What Teachers Need to Know

Colin Harrison

© United Kingdom Reading Association and Colin Harrison

The Teaching of Reading: What Teachers Need to Know
(Based on a paper initially prepared for the Scottish Office Education Department)

Author: Colin Harrison

First published 1996

ISBN 1 897638 11 6

Published by
United Kingdom Reading Association,
Unit 2, Station Road,
Shepreth, Nr Royston
Herts. SG8 6PZ
United Kingdom

All rights reserved. No part of this publication may be reproduced, stored in a retrieval system, or transmitted in any form or by any means, electronic, mechanical, photocopying or otherwise, without the prior permission of the United Kingdom Reading Association and/or Colin Harrison.

British Library Catalogue in Publication.
A catalogue record for this book is available from the British Library.

CONTENTS

Book no. 32240112
Subject no. 372.4 /Mar
LIBRARY SERVICES

Section 1: Preface

The aim of this book is to review the research literature relating to the teaching of reading, particularly that which applies to the first year of formal literacy instruction in school. In writing the review, I draw particularly upon studies from the UK, but shall also make use of those from other European countries, from the USA and Canada, and from Australia and New Zealand.

I also make use of perspectives gained from a series of interviews undertaken with Peter Bryant, FRS, Watts Professor of Experimental Psychology at Oxford University, with experienced Primary 1 teachers working in seven schools in two Scottish regions, and with a number of experienced primary heads and reception class infant teachers in England.

If I had been led to structure this book purely from a review of the research literature, it is possible that I might have given too little attention to a number of issues which are perceived as important by teachers of beginning reading, since the research literature gives great (some would argue disproportionate) emphasis to phonological processing and to the teaching of letter-sound relationships, and has much less to say about some other aspects of pedagogy. I shall aim to give the important topics of phonological processing and phonics due attention, but I shall also give space to matters of overall language development, classroom organisation, the development of comprehension, the importance of genre in text, and parents' contributions to the teaching of reading, all of which figured prominently in teachers' own accounts of how they taught reading.

A review of research should be comprehensive, synoptic and objective. I have attempted to make this review comprehensive, but I am aware that in the last ten years alone, over 10,000 papers on beginning reading have been added to the Educational Resource Information Center (ERIC), and that ERIC reviewers scan over 350 journals for articles on reading research. I have attempted to make it synoptic, but I am aware that it is not easy to strike a balance between offering bland generalities and drawing too heavily upon unreplicated individual studies. I have attempted to be objective, but I am acutely aware that what one person sees as balanced, another sees as prejudiced. I recognise that, in these post-structuralist times, some literary theorists find any claim to authorial "objectivity" unacceptable (see, for example, Eagleton, 1983), just as some scientists find claims to scientific "truth" unacceptable (see, for example, Feyerabend, 1978). In my view, while it is possible to attempt to be objective, it is not possible to begin from a value-free position, nor to arrive at a value-free position. My use of the first person is, in part, an acknowledgement of this.

In writing the review, I have attempted to focus on the practical: I have tried to avoid reporting on debates concerning theory, unless there were direct implications for practice and pedagogy related to them. I have also attempted to signal such implications clearly within the text. The order in which the implications are offered is not an order of importance, but follows the order of literature review topics.

I am most grateful to the Scottish Office Education Department for funding which enabled me to undertake this review.

Section 2: Current debates in the teaching of reading: what are the issues?

Perhaps because learning to read is considered so important, by children, by parents, by teachers, by employers, and by politicians, perhaps because beginning reading is big business, and many of those who advocate for reading are investors in that business, debates about reading instruction are often characterised by pugnacious rhetoric, evangelical allegiances and antipathies, and totemistic treatment of gurus. It is as well to clarify from the outset, therefore, which of the many current reading debates this review will touch upon. Although some authors treat all the issues as one, I would suggest that there are five main topics around which controversy has been focused over the past five years. There have been debates about:
(a) reading standards,
(b) the reading process in fluent readers,
(c) the reading process in beginning readers,
(d) the methods by which children should be taught to read, and
(e) the materials with which children should be taught to read.

This book will deal only tangentially with debates on reading standards, but will attempt to offer a perspective on the reading process debates, since these have important implications for instruction. Issues related to methods and materials are of course central to this review.

I tend to share the consensus view of colleagues in the reading research community in the UK and USA, which is that, for two main reasons, researchers are not in a position to make reliable judgments on changes in reading standards over time. The reasons are, first, that definitions of what counts as literacy are neither agreed nor stable, and second, statistical techniques are not available which can provide us with valid and reliable data on reading standards (see Stedman and Kaestle, 1987 for a US perspective; and Cato and Whetton, 1991, for an excellent review of the reliability of local authority testing in

England and Wales). One further interesting paper which deals with some of these issues is the reply by Barry Stierer (1994) to Martin Turner's vitriolic attack on progressivism in reading and the drop in reading standards which Turner felt had been caused by the 'real books' approach to teaching reading (see Turner,1994, for the most readily accessible version of his monograph, which was first published in 1990). Stierer's paper exposes many of the rhetorical and methodological weaknesses in Turner's analysis.

Turner's leaking of local authority test data to the press (The Daily Telegraph, 30th June, 1990) helped to initiate the current debate on reading and the teaching of reading, and his subsequent monograph singled out two theorists, Frank Smith and Kenneth Goodman, as particularly responsible for progressive methods and what he felt was a contingent decline in standards. In some respects, Turner's polemical critique may have diverted the attention of reading specialists from something much more significant, namely that Smith's and Goodman's views on the reading process were already under regular attack from within the reading research community.

The attacks on Smith's and Goodman's views relate to the crucial issue of how fluent readers read. If the reading process in fluent readers is significantly different from that of beginning readers, there are likely to be important implications for pedagogy, and it is in precisely this area that Smith and Goodman have been challenged. Both Smith and Goodman had much to say about the teaching of reading, but Goodman was the more influential in advocating a distinctive model of the reading process.

What's wrong with Goodman's view of the reading process?

Goodman's widely quoted model of reading as a psycholinguistic guessing game (1967, 1976) has had many critics, but among those whom I would regard as the most authoritative and cogent are Stanovich (1986), Rayner and Pollatsek (1989) and Adams (1990).

For an example of a scholarly but less temperate critique, see that of Liberman and Liberman (1992). Their criticisms may be conflated and summarised as follows:

- Goodman's model is poor on detail.
- Good readers are not dependent on context for word recognition.
- Good readers fixate nearly every word as they read.
- Good readers have automatic word recognition.

Let us consider each of these points in turn:

- ***Goodman's model is poor on detail.***

Goodman's model puts great emphasis on the fact that good readers make efficient use of hypothesis-formation and prediction in reading, but the model is vague on details concerning how such information is used. Goodman's model, in fact, is unspecific on details of (a) how 'visual cues' come to be chosen for processing in the first place, and (b) how semantic, syntactic and phonological information is integrated during reading.

- ***Good readers are not dependent on context for word recognition.***

Goodman's model puts great emphasis on the fact that good readers make efficient use of context, but while this is certainly true in a general sense, especially in relation to comprehension, there is one crucial respect in which this emphasis is misleading. Current views of the reading process turn Goodman's model on its head and stress that what differentiates a good reader from a poor reader is not so much that the good reader makes better use of context, but rather that he or she has increasingly less need to do so. The good reader has automatic, context-free word recognition. In other words, when it comes to word recognition, it is the good reader who does not need to use context in order to decide what a word is. The poor reader, by contrast, cannot recognise a word straightaway, and needs to make use of context to aid word recognition. This takes up valuable processing capacity, thus reducing the processing capacity available for comprehension.

• ***Good readers fixate nearly every word as they read.***

Goodman's emphasis on reading as a predictive process led him to suggest that, as a child develops reading skill and speed, he or she 'uses increasingly fewer graphic cues' (Goodman, 1976). In other words, the argument was that fluent readers are more efficient users of minimal cues, and have less need than a beginning reader to sample more than a few features of the visual array. Advances in eye movement technology have made available data from a great many studies which lead us to a somewhat different interpretation of what happens in fluent reading. What is currently thought is that fluent readers fixate nearly every word, and that they do so very rapidly. It is indeed the case that fluent readers are more efficient than poor readers, but it is not the case that they use less visual information, rather that they sample the visual array more quickly, and use fewer resources to do so. Far from skipping over words, fluent readers not only fixate most words (apart from very short ones such as of, to, and, and the) but appear to process the individual letters in each word, even when the word is highly predictable.

• ***Good readers have automatic word recognition.***

Goodman emphasised that the reading process makes intensive use of prediction and hypothesis formation. This is certainly the case, but Goodman's model seems to imply much more conscious processing and hypothesising than is possible if, as we now believe, word recognition occurs in most cases in less than a quarter of a second, and information is integrated before the eye jumps to its next point of fixation. Comprehension and integration of meaning occur in the ways Goodman described, but conscious hypothesis testing is only used as an aid to word recognition when the reader meets a comprehension problem. A reader who was dependent upon scouring the text for forward-acting and backward-acting context cues in order to decide what a word was would read at the speed of someone doing a cloze exercise, and even with a predictable text would only guess correctly about sixty percent of the time.

A model of the reading process which is currently more widely accepted than that of Goodman among reading researchers is the 'Interactive-Compensatory Model' of Keith Stanovich (1984). Stanovich makes the point that reading involves a number of reader interactions with the text, but a crucial one is that which allocates processing capacity. If a reader is reading fluently, relatively less processing capacity is needed for word recognition, and more is freed up for comprehension. But the process is interactive: if problems are encountered with word recognition, there is compensation, and additional resources are allocated to the word recognition part of the process, but at the expense of some of the capacity which would otherwise have been available for comprehension.

Another very important term in current accounts of learning to read is also attributable to Keith Stanovich. This is the 'Matthew effect'. In a celebrated paper, Stanovich (1986) advanced the argument that there was clear longitudinal evidence of a 'rich get richer while the poor get poorer' effect in beginning reading. He produced statistical evidence to demonstrate that children's increase in vocabulary knowledge and reading fluency was exponential rather than linear, and suggested that this implied that educators should place great emphasis on the importance of early success, since a delayed start in literacy led to losses which were in many respects irrecoverable. The reason for the 'Matthew effect' (his term is of course derived from the parable of the talents, from St Matthew's Gospel in the New Testament) is explicable in cognitive terms: it is not simply that reading broadens the vocabulary and increases knowledge; it is also the case that many of the abilities important in beginning reading, such as phonological awareness, spelling and using analogies to decipher words, have bidirectional causal effects. As we shall see in sections 5 and 6, phonological awareness is a causal factor in learning to read, but reading also improves phonological awareness, which itself is not fully developed until about age 8 or 9. These bidirectional learning effects are what lead to the exponential growth in learning, and produce the 'Matthew effect'.

What is the significance of these challenges to Goodman's model?

The first point to stress is that related to word recognition. It is clear that to many cognitive psychologists, what differentiates a good reader from a poor reader is the good reader's superior capacity for rapid, automatic, context-free and accurate word recognition. Many who hold this view would argue, therefore, that helping children to acquire early, rapid and accurate word recognition should be a key goal for teachers. The issue of how to achieve it, however, is complex and challenging. As this review will make clear, a recognition of the importance of rapid word recognition will not lead us back to a 'whole-word' or 'look and say' approach to beginning reading. Neither will it lead us away from emphasising the importance of reading for meaning and reading for enjoyment, using the best available resources.

Many of the challenges to Goodman's model are related to the fact that his account of word recognition was inadequate. Much of what Goodman has written remains important and valuable. His argument that skilled readers make better use of context than poor readers holds true in relation to two areas- the case of beginning readers, and in the crucial area of comprehension; where Goodman is thought to have been wrong is in overgeneralising his argument to the word recognition of fluent readers. Equally, Goodman's emphasis on the importance of stressing that reading is about the search for meaning should not be underestimated, and it is this emphasis which remains the most significant contribution of his perspective.

How, then do fluent readers recognise words?

The answer to this question is much more complicated than used to be thought. Within experimental psychology, the 'dual-route' theory which was held to account for much of word recognition has had to be abandoned. The dual-route theory posited two routes to word recognition: a whole-word route and a sounding-out route. Fluent readers were thought to use the whole-word route most of the time, and the sounding-out route when they encountered an unfamiliar word. This account is very attractive, and fits in well with what we feel we do as readers. But it is wrong. We now know that fluent readers do not process words as 'wholes'. In normal reading, and during each fixation (ie every quarter of a second), fluent readers process individual letters, make use of knowledge of spelling patterns and word patterns, make use of their knowledge of semantic and syntactic constraints, and produce a phonetic version of the text (though this is usually produced after, rather than before, words have been recognised).

As with Goodman's model, the issue which arises is how all these different types of information are called up and integrated. The models of cognitive processing which are currently accepted as assisting us in answering this question are dauntingly complex. Parallel distributed processing (PDP) models are those which are now being used to attempt to understand brain activity, and unlike earlier psychological models, PDP models aim to replicate cognitive processes by modelling the architecture of the brain. Such models begin by recognising that the way the brain functions is not how traditional computers have functioned. Indeed, in this sense, Goodman was right to emphasise that the reading process relies on probabilistic cognitive functioning, rather than on the serial processing of incremental cognitive units. PDP models of cognitive functioning stress that neuron connections in the brain fire much too slowly to work in the ways computers currently operate: the basic hardware of the brain is a million times slower than the basic hardware of the latest serial computers (Rumelhart and McClelland, 1986).

What the brain does, and what computer models can only begin to approximate to, is to operate what amount to hundreds of parallel processing systems. In the human brain, these systems do not seem to function as sets of on-off logic switches, but rather operate and make decisions by a process of cumulative activation, based on fuzzy logic and statistical thresholds- in other words, by prediction and gradual confirmation. As Rumelhart and McClelland, the leaders in PDP research, put it, "brain-style computation ... should be thought of more as settling into a solution than calculating a solution" (1986, Vol 1, p.135). Such an account sounds perfectly compatible with much that Kenneth Goodman wrote, and it is worth bearing this in mind when considering some of the attacks on him which have been launched by cognitive psychologists over the past fifteen years. In all this parallel processing activity, however, it must again be emphasised that the processing of individual words and individual letters within words remain absolutely crucial parts of the reading process.

Implications from Section 2

From this brief review of current insights into the reading process, therefore, we are in a position to identify some implications for pedagogy:

• For a child to become a proficient reader, the following are crucial: automatic, rapid letter recognition automatic, rapid word recognition the ability to use context as an aid to comprehension the ability to use context when necessary as a conscious aid to word recognition

• These needs do not imply a return to 'look and say' approaches, nor do they imply a shift away from the importance of reading for meaning and reading for enjoyment.

Section 3: What beginning readers need to know about language

In the vexed area of initial literacy, there is one matter over which there is little or no disagreement among teachers or researchers, namely that in order to learn to read, a child needs to have a number of abilities and various types of knowledge. First, and most importantly, a reader needs to have the ability to comprehend discourse. The ability to comprehend in one's mother tongue is much more complex an achievement than is commonly recognised. Indeed, in relative terms, understanding speech is thought to be a much more complex and challenging task than decoding print.

Nearly all children can understand speech, but it is worth recalling that while computers currently perform fairly well at word recognition from print, they are much poorer at speech recognition, and even worse at comprehension. Comprehension of speech requires the ability to interpret a semi-continuous stream of elided phonemes which reach the ear at a rate of up to 1000 per minute (Liberman and Liberman, 1992). In order to accomplish the goal of comprehension, it is necessary to recognise words and word boundaries, to understand the meaning or referent of the words, to perceive and comprehend the grammatical relations between the words, and to relate the information in the sentence to a discourse context, then to one's own world knowledge. By the age of 6, most children can do this remarkably well. They have acquired a listening vocabulary of approximately 10,000 words (Miller, 1977), they understand most (but not all) common grammatical forms (see the excellent review of research in this field by Oakhill and Garnham, 1988), and they have a working knowledge of a number of varieties of discourse and linguistic register which they can recognise, comprehend and generate.

To be proficient in all this is a remarkable achievement, but in rehearsing this list of accomplishments one is bound to acknowledge that a child who can understand speech, but who limited in any of these abilities, is bound to face extra difficulties in learning to read. In particular, it is clear that a reader for whom English is a second or third language may be at a great disadvantage, at least initially. Learning to read is a complex cognitive challenge, but it is significantly more difficult for a learner who lacks knowledge in any or all of the following areas: vocabulary, the grammar of the language of instruction (I refer here to procedural rather than declarative knowledge), discourse structure (for example, narrative structure), cultural conventions (for example knowing that wolves eat pigs, or that it is bad manners to steal porridge), and general knowledge (for example knowing that a straw house will be weaker than a wooden house). We shall return to this theme in section 9 of this review.

How important is intelligence in learning to read? The general conclusion from a number of studies is that in the early years IQ and reading are only weakly related (see Stanovich, Cunningham and Feeman, 1984, for a review). A careful longitudinal study by Tumner, Herriman and Nesdale (1988), however, indicated that logical and analytical abilities at age six were highly predictive of subsequent success in reading. This research reminds us that IQ tests measure only part of intelligence, and that there are many aspects of general cognitive abilities which are very important in learning to read. Tumner and his colleagues also found that pupils who were behind on phonological awareness but strong in logical and analytical abilities caught up with their classmates in phonological awareness within a year.

The implications of the correlational data on IQ are important, however. If IQ and reading are only weakly related at age 6 (r=0.35), but more strongly related at age 11 (r=0.6), this suggests a most important insight for teachers, namely that it is not essential to be intelligent in order to learn to read. It may even be that learning to read comes to effect measured intelligence at age 11, although another reason for the increased correlation is that the IQ measures used at age 11 include more of a verbal component.

How important are perceptual skills in learning to read? In a general sense perceptual skills are clearly important, and in the period 1950-1970, many programmes aiming to develop visual memory, visual discrimination, auditory discrimination and auditory-visual integration were developed. Often these programmes were associated with the belief that they would aid in the development of whole-word recognition. However, it is now thought that most, if not all, such programmes were of doubtful pedagogical utility (see Adams, 1990, for a review).

The factor which does seem to be of critical significance in preschooling is the time spent by parents in literacy activity with their children. Adams (1990), in her landmark review of research into beginning reading, calculates the time spent by a 'mainstream' middle-class parent in such activity, and also the time spent by the child watching the literacy-focussed television programme 'Sesame Street'. She estimates that by the age of six, her son will have spent up to 1700 hours having stories read to him, and 1000 hours watching 'Sesame Street', and that many children will have had twice the story-telling time than that given to her son. By contrast, she estimates that in the first year of schooling, her son's teacher will devote 360 hours to literacy instruction, and that less than 18 hours will be individual tuition. Gordon Wells (1985) reported similar research into children's exposure to stories in the preschool years, and cited a range of 0-7000 stories read or heard before beginning school. Clearly, time spent on stories is valuable in a number of respects: it extends imagination, it widens vocabulary, it increases acquaintance with a variety of grammatical and syntactic structures, it increases awareness of story conventions and text structures, and it encourages talk and problem solving.

One other aspect of language development which is worth emphasising is the importance of encouraging children to tell stories, especially when this is linked to dramatic play. Teale (1987), in an excellent review of research into emergent literacy, reported on the value of such activities. Young children in preschool groups dictated stories to their teacher. In the experimental classes, the children were also encouraged to dramatise the stories in teacher-directed group activity. The storytelling was valuable in both groups, but those in which the dramatic play was introduced came to create stories which were both more complex and at the same time more coherent than those of the story-only groups. Teale also reported studies which found that dramatic play in the preschool class increased subsequent reading comprehension, and appreciation of literature. In his view this was a compelling argument for introducing dramatic play into children's activities.

But naturally, these literacy activities are only a part of what a child will learn in a supportive environment; much of what will be learned will be directly related to print, and in the next section of this review we shall turn to research on this aspect of what children need to know before they can learn to read.

Implications from Section 3

- Children learning to read need to possess of all the following:
    - vocabulary knowledge
    - knowledge of the grammar of the language of instruction
    - knowledge of discourse structure (e.g, narrative structure)
    - knowledge of cultural conventions
    - general knowledge

- It is not essential to be of average intelligence or above in order to learn to read; indeed, it may even be the case that those who learn to read early will become more intelligent, in that reading may increase their verbal reasoning ability.

- Preschool literacy activity is enormously important; it extends imagination, widens vocabulary, increases knowledge of grammatical structures and teaches cultural conventions, discourse structures and problem solving.

- Engagement in preschool dramatic play can extend the development of the abilities listed in the previous paragraph.

Section 4: What beginning readers need to know about print

There has been solid research since the 1960s which has shown that the best single predictor of reading achievement at the end of the first year of literacy instruction is the ability to recognise and name the letters of the alphabet upon entry to school (Bond and Dykstra, 1967; Wells and Raban, 1978; Blatchford et al., 1987).

It has also been shown, however, that simply teaching children the alphabet does not guarantee that they will rapidly develop literacy skills. The relationship between letter knowledge and reading is not a simple causal one. Knowledge of the alphabet may, of course, be little more than an indicator of general literacy support in the home, but other explanations are possible. It is now thought that letter knowledge is indeed causally related to learning to read, but that such knowledge becomes valuable only when it is deep and automatised. Just as word recognition is most valuable when it is automatic, and takes up only a minor amount of processing capacity, so letter knowledge is valuable when it is deep and automatic. There are two somewhat different ways in which this letter knowledge then comes to be used: first in establishing sound-symbol correspondences, and second in the rapid recognition and processing of letters and letter strings during reading.

Letter knowledge is, of course, only one of a number of print-related concepts which are valuable to the beginning reader. Marie Clay's Concepts of Print Test, which she developed as part of her research into beginning reading and reading failure (Clay, 1979), requires the reader to demonstrate knowledge of aspects of a printed text such as the following: orientation- being able to place a book the correct way up; recognising that it is print which carries the verbal message; understanding that print is read from left to right; locating the first and last parts of the story; recognising that the top line of print is read first; understanding that the page number is not part of the story.

Interestingly, some researchers have found that scores on Clay's tests do not always predict future reading ability too accurately. Perhaps one reason for this is that such knowledge soon becomes widely known to children, so even those who are slow to grasp the alphabetic principle are able to score fairly well on a concepts of print test. Clay herself argues that her test is best used for individual diagnosis and remediation in the first year of instruction rather than for norm-referenced assessment. She goes so far as to suggest that if teachers wish to make use of the overall scores, the best way might be to make up their own school table of standardised scores (Clay, 1979, p.31).

The other very important aspect of preschool print awareness to be considered in this section is what is generally called environmental print. As children become aware of print, they are able to point out words which are part of their environment. They come to know that the letters on a Smarties tube say the word 'Smarties', and that the word under the famous twin yellow arches says 'Macdonalds', and so on. Sometimes they guess incorrectly from context, and say 'Coke' instead of 'Pepsi', but in general a very important principle is being established, namely that the letters make sounds, and that the sounds make a word. This understanding is enormously important, of course, but what exactly do children think the relationship is between the letters and the word? It is tempting to make the assumption that what is going on here is essentially an early attempt at whole-word recognition. After all, the child seems to making a global sound-symbol association. However, what researchers now think is that children do not recognise words as 'wholes', neither at this early stage nor later.

What Philip Gough and his co-workers have argued compellingly (Gough and Hillinger, 1980; Gough, Juel and Griffith, 1992) is that what we call 'whole-word' recognition is in fact based not so much upon associations between sounds and global visual arrays, but rather between sounds and letters or letter strings. In other words, they argue that, in English at least, it is inaccurate and misleading to assume that words are ever processed and stored as 'wholes', without attention to letters or letter strings. Rather, they argue that right from the start, children are learning to associate letters and letter strings with parts of words. The visual cues which readers use, even in the early stages, are usually visually distinctive letters or letter groups. Initially these may not be directly associated with sounds, but this association is soon built up, whether the context is environmental print, or whether it is in the first book of a 'look and say' scheme. Initially, this 'logographic' reading is fairly inaccurate. It represents the first stage in reading, but it is a very rudimentary one; it is alphabetic, but without phonological associations. This is understandable, but Gough's view is that the child's reading will remain inaccurate unless he or she develops a more systematic basis for storing and accessing letter and letter-group information. In his view, environmental print is important in early development, but poor as a basis for establishing generalised procedures for deciphering print later on.

Implications from Section 4

• Children need to be able to recognise and name the letters of the alphabet, but simply teaching children the alphabet does not guarantee that they will develop literacy skills; in order to be useful, that knowledge needs to be deep and automatised.

• Concepts of print are important, but a concepts of print test only predicts reading ability in very young children; after a year of literacy instruction such a test does not differentiate between good and poor readers.

• What we have called 'whole-word recognition' is a misnomer. Words are not recognised as 'wholes'; even 'look and say' responses are logographic, ie they make use of alphabetic knowledge, but do not use phonological associations.

• Environmental print is important in the early stages, but it is a poor basis for establishing generalised procedures for decoding at later stages.

Section 5: How children learn to read

One surprising finding of my personal research in primary schools is that the very teachers who have the greatest responsibility for initial literacy are often very hesitant when invited to explain how children learn to read. Such teachers are often very experienced, and because of the importance of their job usually have the trust and respect of their head teacher. Such teachers are usually eloquent and fluent when explaining what methods they use, and how they organise a class of children who are new to school and desperately keen to learn to read. Many times, however, I have asked such teachers, after they have told me how they organise and how they teach, just how it is that the many activities they provide enable a child to learn to read, and they typically claim to find it enormously difficult to answer. Interestingly, while hesitating, and saying that they are not sure that they can explain to me how a child comes to learn to read, they use the same expression: in Scotland, and in England, teachers have said the same thing- 'it just clicks'.

I am not sure that highly experienced professionals do not understand how children come to learn to read; I have an open mind on that issue. It is certainly possible that they might feel intimidated or vulnerable, or that they feel they lack the appropriate discourse for describing the processes which occur. But I do think that the use of the verb 'to click' is an interesting one. It suggests the integration of a number of processes, and it suggests a fairly rapid and even spontaneous integration and acceleration of those processes. My feeling is that, even in books on teaching reading, very rarely is an explicit attempt made to describe what occurs at the very important moment when 'it clicks'.

Naturally, different teachers may mean different things when they refer to 'the click', but the essential point is that the expression is used to refer to the child gaining some autonomy in reading, in particular that the child has become able to work out new grapheme-phoneme correspondences for himself or herself. As I have indicated already, for most (though not all) children, this does not occur spontaneously, it occurs following a good deal of teacher encouragement, support and intervention. The first stage on the way to autonomy is imprecise, and may be described as logographic. In other words, while the child may be able to recognise the word 'fun', that word knowledge is unanalysed: the learning is alphabetic, in that it involves a recognition of the letters in the word, but initially at least, a child does not grasp the phonological aspect of the alphabetic principle. One should note at this point that the term 'alphabetic' is used by Gough (Gough, Juel, and Griffith, 1992) to refer to the awareness of letters and letter strings, while other researchers use it to imply an awareness of the letter-phoneme principle.

The crucial part of the process of learning to read, then, is the ability to work out and recognise previously unrecognised words. In order to be able to accomplish this, the child needs to have a number of abilities, one of the most important of which is a phonological ability, and this ability is often referred to by the term 'phonological awareness'. The term 'phonological awareness' has come to prominence over the past ten years, and is particularly associated with the research of Peter Bryant, Lynette Bradley and Usha Goswami. Some of the most significant insights into how children learn, or fail to learn to read, are attributable to the work of Bryant and his associates, who, particularly over the past six years, have published a series of studies whose range and importance is difficult to overestimate. Bryant's work with Bradley on amassing evidence pointing to a causal link between awareness of rhyme and subsequent success in reading is of great significance (Bryant, Bradley, MacLean and Crossland, 1989), but other studies with Usha Goswami (Goswami and Bryant, 1990) on how children use their phonological awareness to construct analogies are equally important. More recently, he and his co-workers have conducted important studies of the relationship between children's syntactic awareness and their subsequent ability to make use of context in reading, into the reading-spelling connection, and into the relationship between socioeconomic status and reading development, all of which are of great importance.

What is phonological awareness, and why do some theorists seem to prefer to use the term 'phonemic awareness'? The answer is that while some commentators seem to use the terms interchangeably, 'phonological awareness' is now generally taken to be the wider term. It refers to children's ability to manipulate mentally the sounds which make up words. The term 'phonemic awareness' is increasingly used to refer to a subset of that skill, namely the ability to recognise and manipulate phonemes, the smallest chunks of the sounds which make up words. The difference is important, since on this analysis children develop some general phonological awareness months or years before they develop the more refined phonemic awareness, and that it is phonological awareness which is now thought to be not only a strong predictor of future success in reading, but a causal factor in that process.

Phonological awareness does not involve any knowledge of print; it is about recognising, segmenting and manipulating sounds. For example, a person needs to have phonological awareness in order to identify which of the following three words does not rhyme: cat, bat, leg. Bryant showed not only that phonological knowledge predicted future success in reading, but that children's knowledge of nursery rhymes at age 3 contributed independently to their success. As we have noted, correlational studies can be challenged if a researcher claims a causal relationship between the variables under examination, but Bryant's studies were of two types. He established the connection through careful correlational analysis, using multiple regression to partial out other possible factors, such as IQ, socioeconomic status, and finally showed a strong link between nursery rhyme knowledge and subsequent success in reading. He also initiated intervention studies in which he set out specifically to develop phonological awareness in the preschool years, using nursery rhymes and other approaches, and showed that children went on to learn to read successfully.

How do children make use of their phonological awareness? This question was answered by Goswami and Bryant, and by a number of other groups working in parallel studies in the US and Australia (see Gough, Ehri and Trieman, 1992, for a comprehensive review). After operating initially at a logographic stage, during which children recognise words using letters or letters groups but not sound-symbol connections, children develop their ability to connect up the sounds in part of a word with the letter or letters which go with that sound, and become able to use this knowledge in a new context, by analogy. Analogical reasoning is of great importance in this process, and it works initially with two phonological units, the first phoneme in a word (often referred to as the 'onset'), and the remainder of the word (often referred to as the 'rime': goat, coat and vote all rhyme, but only goat and coat share the same rime, oat). The issue of how the sounds and words are segmented is of critical importance, both for learning and for pedagogy.

Goswami and Bryant argue that at this stage children are not capable of making full phonemic discriminations throughout a word; but they are able to differentiate between onset and rime, and that is what enables them to make their first analogical decisions. In fact, children found it easier to draw analogies using information in the latter part of a word, the rime, initially. For example, if they knew how to say 'beak' they could deduce how the word 'weak' should be pronounced. But to begin with, five-year-olds were not able to learn how to make more complex analogies, for example deducing how to say 'bean' if they knew 'beak'. This led Goswami and Bryant to their suggestion that early analogies are based on the rime, and are only made when a spelling unit (such as '-eak') corresponded with a speech unit. We can see immediately why a sensitivity to rhyme would be of value to a child beginning to decipher print through the use of analogy: if the initial segmentation which children operate is based on the rhyming parts of words, it is not surprising that this facet of phonological awareness is a good predictor of early success with reading.

Goswami's initial experiments on analogical learning were with short lists of single words, but she went on to obtain the same results with experiments recording children's use of analogies in authentic reading tasks. Goswami and Bryant also make the point that some complex analogies are only grasped after children have been reading with reasonable fluency for many months. The main stages, however, are these:
a) analogies using spelling sequences and speech units based on the rime (beak-> weak)
b) analogies using the onset (trim-> trap)
c) analogies using phonemes within the rime (beak-> bean)

Goswami and Bryant were not the first researchers to seek evidence for children's use of analogies in early reading, but their work was particularly imaginative. A great deal of subtlety went into their experiments, and eliminated possible flaws or confounding variables which had weakened earlier studies.

Most researchers agree that phonological awareness is not spontaneously acquired by all children. Furthermore, a number of studies suggest that teaching phonological awareness is especially helpful for 'at risk' children (see Adams, 1990, pp328-332, for a review). The approaches which have been used to develop phonological awareness include the following:

• Pre-print: involving the children a variety of activities and games which include rhyming, poetry, singing, tapping, clapping; segmenting sentences into words, and making judgments about words and word length; rhymed stories; placing together objects which begin with the same sound; rhyming speech ("speak in rhyme, all the time"); dancing to syllabic rhythms; speaking like a 'Dalek' (one-syll-a-ble-at-a- time); identification of (but not using these actual terms) onset, rime, phonemes within a rime.

• Print-related: using words made from plastic alphabetic letters, in order to help children to see how easily changing one letter can make an analogous word, beginning with a word the child knows (see Bryant and Bradley, 1985, for a full account).

There is a massive literature on the issue of segmentation, i.e. how we teach children to split up words when developing analogies, and I have necessarily reported it selectively, and with a focus on findings with reasonably clear pedagogical implications.

Following Bryant, there would seem to be compelling reasons for teaching initial segmentation along onset-rime lines, followed by segmenting which keeps to the principle of using articulatory units linked to letter groups, in other words linking spelling patterns to sounds which the child is able to discriminate. By implication, too much emphasis on letter-phoneme relationships at the earliest stages might be premature and profitless.

Marie Clay (1979) offers detailed prescription on word analysis, and stresses the importance of individual help in this vital skill. She, too, makes the point that good readers store and process letters in groups rather than one at a time, and while emphasising the importance of initial and final letters, also advocates giving attention to large rather than small letter strings, from the outset, wherever possible. It is worth stressing that Clay offers 34 teaching suggestions for teaching word analysis, and that segmentation is, of course, only one part of the matter.

One further comment about the teaching of sound-symbol relationships: in her influential review of how children learn to read, Adams (1990) makes a point that at first seems surprising. She stresses that the reason phonics programs are effective is not because they teach children to sound words out. The most important gains from phonics instruction, in her view, are much more directly related to fluent reading: in her view, what a child is able to do as a result of successful learning from phonics instruction is to recognise letters, spelling patterns and whole words effortlessly and automatically, and this is the key to fluent reading.

In reviewing the literature, I have found plenty of caveats about teaching children letter names; it seems clear that without a fairly thorough knowledge, and without phonological awareness, knowledge of letter names is of little use. I have found many caveats warning that the teaching of phonics (i.e. the explicit teaching of sound-symbol relationships) may be profitless, unless the learner has phonological awareness, and unless the other important aspects of reading for enjoyment and meaning are stressed. But I have yet to encounter an account of ineffectual and misplaced evangelism in relation to the teaching of phonological awareness. Perhaps such studies have yet to be reported. A more optimistic analysis, however, might be to suggest that our understanding of the importance of phonological awareness has come at a time and in a climate which is determined to stress the importance of a wholistic approach to beginning reading, a climate in which many reading specialists, whether teachers or researchers, are beginning to adopt less adversarial stances towards each other. Certainly, in his own work, Bryant has gone so far as to conclude one of his papers with a statement that in his view there is nothing incompatible in seeking to develop phonological awareness within a 'real books' approach to teaching reading. To advocates of phonics teaching, and to advocates of an approach whereby children are introduced to meaningful passages at the first opportunity, Bryant suggests that a '...controversy is unnecessary. Both views are right' (Rego and Bryant, 1993).

Implications from Section 5

• In order to work out previously unrecognised words, a child needs to have a number of abilities, one of the most important of which is phonological awareness, which is the ability to manipulate mentally the sounds which make up words.

• Developing phonological awareness seems to be related, in many children at least, to their familiarity with nursery rhymes.

• Phonological awareness can be taught (though it is by no means certain that all children will profit equally from instruction in it) through the following: activities and games which include rhyming, poetry, singing, tapping, clapping; segmenting sentences into words, and making judgments about words and word length; rhymed stories; placing together objects which begin with the same sound; playing games with rhyming speech ("speak in rhyme, all the time"); dancing to syllabic rhythms; speaking like a 'Dalek' (one-syll-a-ble- at-a-time); identification of (but not using these actual terms) onset, rime, phonemes within a rime.

• Learning to recognise previously unknown words through analogies seems to occur in three main stages, and the third stage is not reached for many months: (1) using spelling sequences and speech units based on the rime, (beak-> weak): (2) using the onset (trim-> trap) : (3) using phonemes within the rime (beak-> bean)

• The goal of teaching children sound-symbol relationships is not so that they can sound words out; it is to facilitate rapid and automatic letter and word recognition.

• There is nothing incompatible or inconsistent in a teaching approach which emphasises both phonics (letter-sound relationships) and 'real books'.

Section 6: The reading-writing-spelling connection

It is perhaps worth emphasising the point that one of the tenets of the 'whole language' movement, namely that reading and writing should be taught at the same time (see Ashworth, 1992, for a typical position statement), is also widely accepted in cognitive psychology. A good deal of research has supported the view that developments in reading, writing and spelling are intimately connected, though, as we shall see, some skills develop in clusters. In developing this point, I want to refer in some detail to a study conducted by Mommers (1987) in Holland. The study was based on a 5-year longitudinal enquiry, and was much more thorough than most which have been conducted in the UK. The study also offers a bridge to section 7, since it compared the effects of two reading schemes, one with a relatively greater emphasis on whole-word reading, and one with a relatively greater emphasis on phonics. Both schemes were employed in 12 classes, in a variety of schools, so Mommers felt reasonably able to generalise from the results.

What Mommers reported was that both approaches yielded remarkably similar results at the end of the first year of literacy instruction. In both sets of classrooms two factors predicted success in reading, as measured at the end of the school year; one was an auditory factor (this was essentially phonological awareness), but even more powerful as a predictor was a general factor, which Mommers called conceptual knowledge. His conclusion from this was that while developing phonological awareness and teaching phonics is important, developing concept formation is also essential to assist reading development. Mommers also found that after as little as 4 months formal instruction, children's speed of decoding words and ability in spelling had developed differently, and could be distinguished empirically. The fascinating finding concerned the direction of the prediction: in the case of both groups, those using the scheme with greater emphasis on look and say, and those using the scheme with greater emphasis on phonics, it was the ability to spell which predicted decoding speed (and thus decoding ability), rather than the other way round.

The implications of this are profound: they suggest that learning to spell early gives Dutch children an advantage in relation to subsequent reading development. Indeed, in the case of the 'look and say' group, spelling ability after four months of reading instruction was a better predictor of reading comprehension than was the ability to decode words. This should not surprise us, if it is the case that spelling ability indicates a general ability to analyse a word into phonemes and match those phonemes to letters, it is just this ability which will be needed in construing new words that are met later in the year. Speed of decoding words which are in one's sight vocabulary may not be a good predictor of subsequent decoding of words which are not.

This research took place with Dutch children, and they were learning a language which is more phonologically regular than English. We might therefore predict for children in the UK, that initial decoding would rely to a greater extent than is the case in Holland on a logographic (or at least a partially logographic) route, simply because so many frequent words are irregular. Nevertheless, as Gough has pointed out (Gough, Juel, and Griffith, 1992), when children are beginning to find their feet as independent readers, it is precisely on unfamiliar words, which are more likely to be lower in absolute word frequency and more phonologically regular, that they will need to use their skills at deciphering and sounding out and drawing analogies - skills that require very similar abilities to those involved in spelling. It may seem surprising that I choose to devote detailed attention to this study, carried out in another country and another language, but the study has a number of attributes which make it worth reporting: it is based in the classroom; it is longitudinal, and (as Bryant's classroom studies did) makes use of the LISREL statistic to attempt to isolate causal factors rather than simply reporting correlations; it compares two reading schemes, one with a look-say emphasis, one with more attention to phonics instruction. The LISREL analysis produces flow-diagram-like models which link a number of variables, or groups of variables, on which longitudinal data have been gathered, and offers an indication of how well these data fit a causal explanation of performance over time.

Mommers is cautious about making extravagant claims for this study; he reminds us that building LISREL models is an art as much as a science, but nevertheless, he does identify implications from his own study:

a) phonological awareness has a significant effect on the early stages of reading acquisition, and therefore children should be introduced to phonemic segmentation before reading instruction starts; this could be accomplished in a variety of ways, through rhyme, sorting objects or spoken words by their initial sounds, and so on;

b) however, initial instruction should not concentrate too exclusively upon auditory aspects of the reading process- special attention should be also given to teaching general aspects of development- concept formation, schemata and overall language comprehension;

c) decoding, spelling and reading comprehension were separately identifiable as competences, and this suggested that specific teaching time should continue to be given to each, initially, but also during first two years of formal schooling.

More recently, Rego and Bryant (1993) have come to parallel conclusions in their study of how children come to learn to spell. They reported a 'remarkable specificity' in different areas within reading and spelling: there was a strong predictive relationship between phonological skills and the later ability in invented spelling, but a weak relationship between phonological skills and later ability to use context in reading. What they argue is that both sets of skills play an important part in reading, but that they develop differently. The implication from this is clear: both sets of abilities should be a part of the pedagogy of reading. As was emphasised at the end of section 5, there are sound research-based reasons for adopting an eclectic approach to reading instruction.

Implications from Section 6

• Developing phonological awareness is important, but so is developing conceptual knowledge.

• Spelling ability is a better predictor of subsequent reading ability than is the ability to recognise words. This may be because initial word recognition is logographic, but subsequent development depends upon phonological and analogical skills, which are more likely to be assessed in a spelling test.

• Instruction in phonological awareness should include work on segmentation of words, as well as rhyming activities.

• It seems likely that specific activities to develop word analysis, spelling and understanding will each be valuable, since the three sets of abilities develop differently in certain respects.

Section 7: The content and organisation of reading instruction

What effect does the method used have in determining how rapidly or how successfully children learn to read? This is a key question for this review to address, and yet it is clear, even before we attempt an answer, that there appear to be national and ideological differences in how researchers approach this issue. The Bullock Report (DES, 1975) conducted survey research into methods of teaching reading, but concluded that research was not capable of identifying more effective methods: 'there is no one method, medium, approach, device or philosophy that holds the key to the process of learning to read' (p.521). Instead, the report offered the view that 'the teacher is the biggest single factor for success in learning to read.' (p.212). This emphasis on the teacher's role and importance is understandable, especially when one considers the influence of educators such as James Britton on the Bullock committee's deliberations, but even this commonsense view is challenged by some (notably in a somewhat notorious paper by Gray, 1979, in which it is argued that research methods are too crude to identify any effect the teacher might have).

What is perhaps surprising in the Bullock report's stance is the implied marginalisation of large-scale studies of reading methods which had been undertaken in the 1960s. Such studies (reviewed by Chall, 1967, and followed by the massive cooperative reading projects coordinated and reported by Bond and Dykstra, 1967) gave weight to a 'code-emphasis' approach. In other words, the differences were not great, but broadly speaking, researchers found in favour of phonics, though Bond and Dykstra were much more conservative than Chall in making this claim. There remained, however, many problems with the large-scale studies. Controls over what the teachers actually taught are weak in such studies, and if such controls are weak in the USA, the results of the studies might be even more difficult to generalise to the UK, where teachers traditionally implement their own programme, making eclectic use of any reading scheme available.

The results of UK-based research are equivocal. Nearly all the early large-scale studies (such as those of Joyce Morris, 1966) have subsequently been questioned on methodological grounds, and the British tradition of paying little attention to research findings in making curriculum decisions has not contributed to climate in which such research has been encouraged.

HMI reports relating to methods of teaching reading in England and Wales have been confident in tone, but based, in part at least, upon impressionistic data which is not available to the rest of the academic community for inspection. One is never certain whether to interpret these HMI reports as based upon solid data or rather as having the status of 'pools panel' results for football matches - namely a best guess from the experts as to what one would expect to find, were one to actually carry out systematic research.

The HMI report 'The Teaching and Learning of Reading in Primary Schools' (DES, 1990) is a case in point. Information such as the following seems entirely useful and in all probability reliable: '...there is no evidence of teachers and schools rushing into a single method of teaching reading. The great majority of teachers, almost 85%, used a blend of methods to teach initial reading skills...(section 14(v))'. Members of the inspectorate keep careful notes, and one is willing to trust that this figure is reliable. By contrast, within the same paragraph, the authors offer the following: 'There was clear evidence that adherence to a single approach, whatever the particular method, hindered the children's reading development.' What sort of 'clear evidence' would a member of the research community regard as adequate in this context? It is difficult to imagine any basis on which an HMI could identify unequivocal evidence to support or indeed confound this claim, within the time constraints of a school inspection, and yet the claim implies that such evidence was available, from a number of sites, and that it all led towards one conclusion. Identifying low reading standards is difficult enough; identifying a causal link between pedagogy and reading attainment is an even more demanding and long-term challenge.

Suppose, for example, that inspectors found a heavy emphasis on 'real books' coinciding with low reading attainment in a number of schools. How confident could one be of the direction of causality in such a case? It could be, for example, not that a 'real books' approach was leading to low reading standards, but that poor pre-school reading skills (vocabulary, concepts of print, phonological awareness, etc.) were causing the teachers to seek an approach to reading in which failure was minimised, authentic children's literature valued, and children were not demoralised by learning that they were still on 'Book One' of a scheme after nine months. Unless 'value added' research methods were used, inspectors would have little evidence on which to make confident assertions about underachievement in reading, and even if they had such data, there are at least three possible sources of variation within schools- a whole-school effect, a teacher effect, and a methods or materials effect- any or all of which could have contributed to the children's attainment.

One enormously important matter in school effectiveness research, upon which there is fair measure of agreement, is that a child's background (intelligence, prior learning, home background, parents, etc) contributes approximately 85% to what is achieved in school; the other 15% is contributed by schooling. Of this about 5% is generally held to be a school factor, 7% a teacher factor, and as little as 3% a method factor (Gray, 1979; Barr, 1984; Adams, 1990). In this respect, the Bullock report was perhaps correct: the teacher is more important than the method, and while methods matter, one implication for administrators is that professional development for teachers is critical; it may produce greater gains than improving methods and schemes.

Large-scale longitudinal studies of reading methods are expensive and complex to run, and after five years, one may be left with the impression, even with the more careful controls and more subtle analytical methods of recent studies, that the results are not particularly illuminating. One of the most careful relatively recent studies of reading methods, for example, was the five-year project of Lesgold, Resnick and Hammond (1985), who in a very detailed report compared inner-city children's learning to read using two different approaches, and a two age-group cohorts. One method emphasised a global approach, with a basal reading programme (which included a strong emphasis on stories) plus small-group reading in similar-ability groups. The other approach emphasised individualised programs to develop word decoding skills and comprehension, specially developed in the University of Pittsburg. Interestingly, after extensive research, Lesgold and his co-workers found that the children using the regular basal scheme learned to read just as successfully as those in the individualised programme. They concluded that there are multiple pathways to reading efficiency, and that neither programme was totally effective, since about 15 percent of the children in each group failed to learn to read fluently after two years instruction.

What seems remarkable is that the programmes were not combined, and this is precisely what is being attempted in the latest US reading schemes (Hoffman, et al, 1994). Hoffman and his 9 co-researchers have analysed the content, structure, methods and philosophy of all five major reading schemes which were recommended for adoption in 1993 in the state of Texas. What they found is interesting: all five new schemes are very similar. Indeed, they are much more similar to each other than they are to the schemes which preceded them, even those schemes which came from the same publisher. In some respects, this is not surprising; the schemes were written to meet the criteria published in an invitation to tender (in Texas, this is a 'Proclamation') in 1990. The Proclamation specified that in order to be considered for state adoption, a scheme would need to include (among many other requirements) the following:

- opportunities to read connected text, not just workbooks
- a 'pluralistic' approach to literature

- unabridged literature
- opportunities to develop reading practice
- integration of reading with speaking, listening and writing
- systematic development of phonological awareness

Such is the influence of Texas textbook adoption procedures that all five major publishers completely revised their reading schemes to meet these criteria. Other new features were a greater inclusion of 'real books' (called 'trade books' in the US) as an integral part of the schemes, and on multiple rereading of stories. Also, strictly controlled vocabulary was much less evident, and while the total number of running words in most schemes was reduced, the total number of different words was increased. Texts with repeated patterns of rhyme and rhythm were more than doubled.

Hoffman is cautious rather than optimistic about the new schemes. He points out that teachers in Texas might feel uneasy with schemes which reduce the emphasis on skills worksheets and increase the emphasis on teacher-led discussion, the use of big books, guided reading, and so on. The schemes imply more teacher autonomy, and while this may be good for many teachers, it could be threatening for others.

What has been happening in the US has many parallels in the UK. No fewer than seven major reading schemes are due to be launched during 1994, and there appears to be a high degree of commonality among them. While there will no doubt remain a residual house style effect, it seems likely that most of the new schemes, while being much less extensive than their US counterparts, will come close to meeting the Texan criteria, with a firm emphasis on a 'real books' component and reading for enjoyment, as well as an emphasis on developing phonological awareness followed by explicit teaching of phonics.

In such a climate, it seems likely that Hoffman's caution is justified.

In the US, workbook and skills-based instruction may have contributed to a situation in which the teacher's influence on the reading development of her students was diminished. In the 1990s, and in a climate in which reading for enjoyment is valued, the teacher's influence seems bound to be considerable.

The issue here is concerned with how children learn, and the part played by those who model reading behaviours. What is potentially enormously valuable in the use of big books, for example, is that the teacher and other children in the class offer a model to a learner of how to read, and indeed how to understand a book. The value of big books is precisely the same as the value of DARTs activities in the later years of reading development (Lunzer and Gardner, 1984): they make public an externalisation of the internal processes of reading, from which a less fluent reader can observe and learn.

It is for this reason that a teacher sharing a big book with a class, or reading the same book with six children once or twice a week, can make an enormous difference to the amount of literacy instruction given to the children in her class. In the light of research discussed earlier, this modelling of reading and reading processes should include attention to all aspects of texts, from top-down prediction of story and vocabulary, to bottom-up attention to punctuation, concepts of print, and features of words on the page. No teacher would wish to attempt all these simultaneously, but the point is that direct teaching is valuable and essential, and that it is much more valuable if it is taught in a context which the child will be able to meet again when rereading a favourite book. 'Each, Peach, Pear, Plum' is a delightful book, and well worth reading for enjoyment from age 3. If a teacher uses the big book version to draw attention to explicit points about the text (whether this teaching refers to story structure or to the use of capital letters for names), that teaching will be reinforced when the child reads the book at home or in the book corner.

One point to emphasise here is the importance of rereading familiar books. Parents (and therefore some teachers) worry about seeing a child bring a favourite book home more than once. Our current understanding of reading processes would emphatically support the principle of rereading familiar books, for as well as increasing enjoyment and motivation, rereading familiar books offers the safest environment for a child to work on transferring words that can be slowly deciphered using analogical knowledge to their bank of words that can be recognised rapidly, accurately and automatically. Without such practice, children may move on too fast to a harder book, and experience reading as a succession of painfully slow deciphering tasks, which would decrease motivation and hamper the development of rapid word-recognition skills.

We must give some attention in this section of the review to the matter of teachers hearing children read. This practice, though understandably regular and widespread, has been questioned by experts who are uncertain of its benefits. Hazel Francis (1987), in review article which is not unsympathetic towards teachers, suggests that there is a need for a clearer understanding of the intentions and pedagogical goals of hearing children read. She hints that in their desire to avoid making the experience an unpleasant one for children, teachers hold back from correcting, and thus from explicit teaching, and that this is perhaps what leads others to see the practice as limited and limiting.

Perhaps one answer would be for the teacher to adopt a range of goals for different occasions, rather than a single strategy. If the practice of hearing a child read for five minutes each week were redefined in terms of five minutes individualised instruction each week, a different and more effective use of this precious time might be possible. This might sometimes be the traditional approach of listening with encouragement and occasional prompting or word-supply (the modal procedure), but on other occasions might focus on silent reading and inference, or might emphasise accuracy more than fluency. Aiming to cycle through a set of perhaps four types of individual procedures such as these might be liberating for the teacher, and might offer an escape route from what for some teachers is a somewhat tyrannising procedure, which leaves her feeling guilty for not offering as much explicit help to the child as she feels is really called for.

Reading teachers are faced with a dilemma. On the one hand, they know that for some things, such as letter-sound relationships, explicit teaching is valuable for children. Equally, they are aware, just as Vygotsky has emphasised, that children can learn only when they are ready, when they are at what Vygotsky called the Zone of Proximal Development. Even then, children can only learn when what is presented is easy to understand, and is offered in the right way. We know that only a small percentage of children learn to read spontaneously, although once they have learned, they can reinforce that learning on their own, if they are motivated to do so. What is required, therefore, would seem to be a variety of opportunities to learn, regularly presented. Story times offer such opportunities, as do small group reading sessions, as do periods of individual instruction, and all of these are crucial.

In the schools I visited, teachers of beginning readers (quite properly, in my view) regarded story time (which of course these days includes attention to non-fiction texts) as a fundamental part of beginning literacy. All the teachers regarded it as essential to have at least one twenty-minute period of small-group reading per week, and most tried to hear each child read individually once a week. This review is not focussed on learning to write, but of course all teachers treated reading and writing as skills which had to be developed in parallel, and my review of the literature would support this emphasis. It is clear not only that there is a symbiotic relationship between reading and writing, but that for many children learning to write in many respects precedes learning to read, in the sense that it is as they learn to apply their understanding of sound-symbol relationships to composing, they become able to transfer this learning to print, and begin to develop an ability to decipher words using analogies.

I referred briefly above to teachers introducing non-fiction texts into story time. I would wish to concur with those who have argued, as Lunzer and Gardner did (1984), that it is crucial to assist children to come to terms with non-fiction texts, not least because they are in many respects more difficult to comprehend than stories. Non-fiction texts tend to contain more new and therefore unfamiliar words, they contain more new ideas, and they use more unfamiliar text structure than story books (Harrison, 1992). I tend to share the view argued with some force by Martin, Christie and Rothery (1994), that children should be introduced at an early age to a variety of genres of text, and that the teacher should offer some explicit teaching to scaffold the children's learning as they tackle such books.

Implications from Section 7

• It is extraordinarily difficult, without 'value-added' research designs, to assess whether a school's reading attainment is above or below what might be expected on the basis of its intake.

• Even if a school were underachieving, this could be attributable to a school effect, a teacher effect, a methods/materials effect, or any combination of these.

• Research suggests that the teacher does have a significant effect on children's learning; this might imply that working on teachers' professional development might be as important as improving methods or materials.

• New schemes are likely to become less heterogeneous than was the case in the past; if they follow US developments, they are likely to emphasise:
- opportunities to read connected text, not just workbooks
- a 'pluralistic' approach to literature
- unabridged literature
- opportunities to develop reading practice
- integration of reading with speaking, listening and writing
- systematic development of phonological awareness

• If children learn best through observation and modelling of behaviour, the teacher's role in the use of 'big books', and in organising and guiding small-group instruction is likely to be critical.

• Rereading of familiar books is essential to the development of confidence and fluency; many parents (and perhaps some teachers) may need educating in this important area.

• Explicit teaching of different text genres, and of the text structure of non-fiction books, is likely to be very valuable for beginning readers.

Section 8: The role of parents and other care-givers

As we have already indicated, parents make a contribution to children's literacy development which is incalculably important, and sections 3 and 4 above offer at least a partial account of this. Once children are in school, however, what should be the role of parents, volunteers in schools and other care givers in assisting children to learn to read?

This question has recently been posed most trenchantly in a review article by Toomey (1993). Toomey reviews the studies which became celebrated during the 1980s, especially those conducted in Haringey, London, in Belfield, Rochdale, and in Kirklees, in the north of England. His conclusions are important: he argues that there is little evidence that sending books home and encouraging parental involvement will, of itself, lead to reading improvement. In many cases it does, but in his view, the research evidence shows that sending books home does little to help those most at risk of reading failure; it does not help low-competence readers whose parents do not realise how much benefit their help can be, or do not know how to help.

Toomey reported studies which demonstrated that, without help and guidance, parents were much less likely than teachers to praise, to pause and therefore encourage guesses or self-correction, or to give clues if children are hesitant. He suggested that careful thought, and appropriate resources, needed to be given to ensure that this invaluable potential support was channelled effectively. Toomey was supportive of 'Pause-prompt-praise' models of support, and of paired reading, but argued that we lack detailed information concerning how best to implement a cost-effective parent-support programme.

One final point: what applies to parents at home applies at least as strongly to volunteer reading helpers in the classroom. Loenen (1989), in a careful study of 15 helpers in four different schools, found that over two terms, children who had two 30-minute sessions per week with the reading helpers made no significant gains in either reading ability or in self-concept, compared with control groups in each class. This finding might seem astounding, but Loenen had detailed recordings of what the helpers did in their sessions, and she found that the helpers had ignored or forgotten the instructions given to them in the three one-and-a-half-hour training sessions which preceded their helping. They did not encourage the children to read for meaning, and they had arbitrary procedures for supplying words the children did not know. Loenen makes some recommendations for improving matters. She felt that the helpers needed:

- regular feedback and support from professionals;
- active training through modelling and role play;
- instruction in what the class teacher was attempting to achieve in her own literacy teaching.

Implications from Section 8

• When listening to children read, teachers, parents and other care-givers need to know more about when to help, when not to help, and how to intervene; without such knowledge, much of this potentially invaluable support for literacy development may be contributing very little.

• The 'pause-prompt-praise' strategy seems potentially a very useful one to implement in reading support contexts.

• Parents and classroom helpers need:
- regular feedback and support from professionals;
- active training through modelling and role play;
- instruction in what the class teacher was attempting to achieve in her own literacy teaching.

Section 9: Children's reading problems

This review will not deal extensively with the issue of helping those who do not learn to read, but some recent findings on this issue are too important to ignore, not least because they may have implications for all classrooms, and for reading policy at local and national levels.

The paper by Keith Stanovich on the Matthew Effect in reading (Stanovich, 1986), advances the argument that early intervention is essential to prevent cumulative and cyclical failures in learning. As most reading specialists know, Marie Clay's reading recovery programme is designed to offer that early intervention, and it seems important to review briefly the arguments surrounding this work and its evaluation. In my view, a very recent article (Pinnell et al., 1994) answers most of the questions researchers have been asking.

As Clay has repeatedly stressed, reading recovery is not a 'method'; it is a programme of individualised instruction, tailored to meet the needs of each child, and it is usually given after the child has received about a year of initial whole-class instruction in beginning reading, but has not yet begun to read. The programme is expensive: not only does reading recovery require that a child receives half an hour of individual instruction per day for up to 20 weeks, the teacher delivering that instruction needs to have been on a year-long training course. Naturally enough, school administrators ask themselves whether, as Clay insists, it is indeed absolutely essential that a reading recovery teacher should have such expensive training. Equally, administrators and head teachers would wish to know whether such an expensively trained teacher might not be capable of teaching a small group rather than an individual, with equal success.

Pinnell has provided answers to these questions, in a thorough and heavily statistical paper, which sought to meet the stringent requirements of validity and generalisability which bedevil classroom research programmes. Pinnell compared a number of teachers using a variety of remedial approaches. These were (a) individualised 'reading recovery', (b) individualised 'reading success' (this was a literature/whole language programme, with emphasis on literature, writing, and running records; in effect, it was a reading recovery approach, but with teachers trained over two weeks rather than over a whole year), (c) individualised 'Direct Skills' (this was a published course, with an emphasis on phonics), (d) Reading/Writing Group (this was in effect reading recovery, and taught by reading recovery teachers, but in groups), and (e) a control group. The main finding was that only one programme produced statistically significant effects across all schools and on all post-test measures; this was individualised reading recovery. This was also the only treatment which maintained its advantage one year after the original study had been completed.

These results suggest that one-to-one individualised instruction, of itself, even when delivered by experienced teachers, is not enough to steer children who are moving towards reading failure back on track; by contrast, reading recovery does achieve this. In fact, the reading success teachers had received a two-week training course in reading recovery techniques, but this proved not to be enough to lead to an effect matching that of reading recovery. The children in the Reading/Writing Group, which was in effect a small-group version of reading recovery, were the second most successful, and outperformed those of the other individualised programmes. The phonics-based remedial programme, by the way, was the least successful.

There are many ways one may interpret the results of this important study. One is that its results are less conclusive than they appear, since they rely on the assumption that all the teachers were equally talented. However, if it is the case that teachers who volunteer and are accepted for reading recovery training are exceptional, this alone could explain the effects that Pinnell attributes to the reading recovery procedure. Pinnell herself accepts that during the course of the year-long training, teachers are offered an opportunity to observe and reflect on their own practice and the practice of other skilled teachers in a manner which has hitherto been unavailable to them. Teachers observe through one-way mirrors and view videotapes of teaching, and these processes offer a site for problematising and discussing practice which is not available for other teachers. Not surprisingly, these procedures might lead to a deepening awareness of and a more mature reflection on professional skills and procedures. It could be such awareness, rather than the reading recovery procedures, which produced the effect.

Nevertheless, I would argue that offering all teachers an opportunity to engage in the type of critical reflection on their practice which reading recovery training offers is very important, and should be a central component in in-service provision.

Implications from Section 9

• The largest US study of Reading Recovery indicated that it was not possible to achieve sustained success in remediation without giving teachers the full one-year training, and without having individualised instruction.

• This finding might be interpreted as further support for the notion that administrators should put funds into teacher development as well as into extra staffing or additional classroom resources.

Section 10: Conclusions

In preparing and writing this review, I have had in mind from the outset to goal of highlighting implications for policy and practice within each section. In certain sections, some of these implications now appear to me to sound a little tendentious; in other places they read as a succession of relatively minor points - tips for teachers, if you will. I hope that I may be forgiven for this; it seemed on balance that this was a reflection of the research material I have been reviewing, some of which was of immediate practical application, some of which was vast and complex in scale and relevance.

Around me, as I write this final page, I am surrounded by books, journals and papers, many of which contain details of studies which have not been included, even though they might have added usefully to this review. This is because I recognise that a review of the literature is not, and must not be, as full of supplementary argument and detail as a book.

I feel certain that this review will not please all its potential readers, since, as I indicated at the outset, it will appear uneven or partisan in places. Nevertheless, I recognise also that those who formulate policy need information in a form which is ideally more condensed yet more digestible than that in which it originally appeared. I hope that this review, even with its possible faults, serves this purpose in some measure. I appreciate very much having been given to opportunity to write it, and would wish to express my thanks to all those who, directly or indirectly, assisted me in the endeavour.

Bibliography

Adams, M. Jager (1990) Beginning to Read: Thinking and Learning About Print. Cambridge MA: MIT Press.

Ashworth, E. (1992) Children's early excursions into literacy: the need for a comprehensive account of the development of reading, writing and spelling. In Colin Harrison and Martin Coles (eds) The Reading for Read Handbook. London: Routledge.

Barr, R. (1984) Beginning reading instruction: from debate to reformation. In David Pearson (ed) Handbook of Reading Research. New York: Longman.

Blatchford, P., Burke, J., Farquhar, C., Plewis, I and Tizard, B. (1987). Associations between pre-school reading related skills and later reading achievement. British Education Research Journal, 13/1, 15-24.

Bond, G.L. and Dykstra,R. (1967) The cooperative research program in first grade reading instruction. Reading Research Quarterly, 2, 5-142.

Bryant, P.E., Bradley, L.MacLean, M. and Crossland, J. (1989) Nursery rhymes, phonological skills and reading. Journal of Child Language, 16, 407-428.

Bryant, P.E. and Bradley, L. (1985) Children's Reading Problems. Oxford: Basil Blackwell.

Cato, V. and Whetton, C. (1991) An Enquiry into LEA Evidence on Standards of Reading of Seven-year-old Children. London: Department of Education and Science (with NFER)

Chall, J. (1967) Learning to Read: the Great Debate. London: McGraw-Hill.

Clay, M.M. (1979) The Early Detection of Reading Difficulties. London: Heinemann.

DES (1990) The Teaching and Learning of Reading in Primary Schools. London: HMSO.

DES (1975) A Language for Life (The Bullock Report). London: HMSO.

Eagleton, Terry (1983) Literary Theory. Oxford: Basil Blackwell.

Feyerabend, P. (1978) Against Method. London: Verso.

Francis, H. (1987) Hearing beginning readers read: problems of relating practice to theory in interpretation and evaluation. British Educational Research Journal, 13/3, 215-226.

Goodman, K.S. (1967) Reading: a psycholinguistic guessing game. Journal of the Reading Specialist, 6, 126-135.

Goodman, K.S. (1976) Reading: a psycholinguistic guessing game. In H. Singer and R.B.Ruddell (eds) Theoretical Models and Processes of Reading. Newark, Delaware: International Reading Association.

Goswami, U. and Bryant, P.E. (1990) Phonological Skills and Learning to Read. Hove, East Sussex: Lawrence Earlbaum.

Gough, P.B. and Hillinger, M.L. (1990) Learning to read: An unnatural act. Bulletin of the Orton Society, 30, 179-196.

Gough, P.B., Juel, C. and Griffith, P.L. (1992) Reading, spelling and the orthographic cipher. In P.B. Gough, L.C. Ehri, and R. Treiman (eds) Reading Acquisition. Hillsdale NJ: Lawrence Erlbaum Associates.

Gough, P.B., Ehri, L.C. and Treiman R. (eds)(1992) Reading Acquisition. Hillsdale NJ: Lawrence Erlbaum Associates.

Gray, John (1979) Reading progress in English infant schools: some problems emerging from a study of teacher effectiveness. British Educational Research Journal, 5/2, 141-158.

Harrison, C. (1992) Information skills: what are they and how can we teach them? In F. Satow and B. Gatherer (eds) Literacy Without Frontiers. Widnes: UKRA.

Harrison, C., and Coles, M. (1992) The Reading for Real Handbook. London: Routledge.

Hoffman, J.V. (and nine co-authors)(1994) So what's new in the basals? A focus on first grade. Journal of Reading Behavior, 26/1, 47-74.

Lesgold, A., Resnick, L.B. and Hammond, K. (1985) Learning to read: a longitudinal study of word skill development in two curricula. In G.E.MacKinnon and T.G.Waller (eds) Reading Research: Advances in Theory and Practice, Vol. 4. London: Academic Press, 107-138.

Liberman, I.Y. and Liberman, A.M. (1992) Whole language versus code emphasis: underlying assumptions and their implications for reading instruction. In P.B.Gough, L.C.Ehri and R.Treiman (eds) Reading Acquisition. London: Lawrence Erlbaum Associates.

Loenen, A. (1989) The effectiveness of volunteer reading help and the nature of the reading help provided in practice. British Educational Research Journal, 15/3, 297-316.

Lunzer, E.A. and Gardner, K. (1984) Learning from the Written Word. Edinburgh: Oliver and Boyd.

Martin, J.R., Christie, F. and Rothery, J. (1994) Social processes in education: a reply to Sawyer and Watson (and others). In B.Stierer and J.Maybin (eds) Language, Literacy and Learning in Educational Practice. Clevedon: Multilingual Matters.

Miller, G. (1977) Spontaneous Apprentices. New York: Seabury Press

Mommers, M.J.C. (1987) An investigation in to the relation between word recognition, reading comprehension and spelling skills in the first two years of primary school. Journal of Research in Reading, 10/2, 122-143.

Morris, J. (1966) Standards and Progress in Reading. Slough: NFER.

Oakhill, J. and Garnham, A. (1988) Becoming a Skilled Reader. Oxford: Basil Blackwell.

Pinnell. G.S., Lyons, C.A., Deford, D.E., Bryk, A.S. and Seltzer, M. (1994) Comparing instructional models for the literacy education of high-risk first graders. Reading Research Quarterly, 29/1, 8-39.
Rayner, K. and Pollatsek, A. (1989) The Psychology of Reading. Englewood Cliffs, NJ: Prentice Hall.
Rego, L.L.B. and Bryant, P.E. (1993) The connection between phonological, syntactic and semantic skills and children's reading and spelling. European Journal of Psychology of Education, 8/3, 235-246.
Rumelhart, D.E. and McClelland, J.L. (1986) Parallel Distributed Processing. Explorations in the Microstructure of Cognition. Volume 1: Foundations. London: MIT Press.
Stanovich, K.E. (1986) Matthew effects in reading:some consequences in individual differences in reading in the acquisition of literacy. Reading Research Quarterly, 21, 360-406.
Stanovich, K. (1984) The interactive-compensatory model of reading: a confluence of developmental, experimental and educational psychology. Remedial and Special Education, 5, 11-19.
Stanovich, K.E., Cunningham, A.E. and Feeman, D.J. (1984) Intelligence, cognitive skills and early reading progress. Reading Research Quarterly, 19, 278-303.
Stedman, L.C. and Kaestle, C.F. Literacy and reading performance in the United States, from 1880 to the present. Reading Research Quarterly, 22/1, 8-46.
Stierer, B. (1994) 'Simply doing their job?' The politics of reading standards and 'real books'. In B.Stierer and J.Maybin (eds) Language, Literacy and Learning in Educational Practice. Clevedon: Multilingual Matters, 128-138.
Teale, W. (1986) Emergent literacy: reading and writing development in early childhood. In J.E.Readence and R.S.Baldwin (eds) Research in Literacy: Merging Perspectives. Rochester NY: National Reading Conference, 45-74.
Toomey, D. (1993) Parents hearing their children read: a review. Rethinking the lessons of the Haringey Project. Educational Research, 35/3, 223-236.
Tumner,W.E, Herriman, M.L. and Nesdale, A.R. (1988) Metalinguistic abilities and beginning reading. Reading Research Quarterly, 23, 134-158.
Turner, M. (1990) Sponsored Reading Failure. Warlingham, Surrey: IPSET Education Unit.
Turner, M. (1994) Sponsored Reading Failure. In B.Stierer and J.Maybin (eds) Language, Literacy and Learning in Educational Practice. Clevedon: Multilingual Matters, 111-127.
Wells, G. (1985) Pre-school literacy-related activities and success in school. In D. Olsen, N. Torrance and A. Hildyard (eds) Literacy, Language and Learning: The Nature and Consequences of Reading and Writing, New York: Cambridge University Press.
Wells, C.G. and Raban, E.B. (1978) Children Learning to Read. Final Report to Social Science Research Council, University of Bristol

United Kingdom Reading Association

The professional association for those concerned with the teaching of language and literacy

UKRA is an association of teachers and educationalists especially interested in the teaching of reading, writing and language. Membership of UKRA brings many benefits including:

Termly issues of *Reading* and *Language and Literacy News*, both containing interesting and practical articles on all aspects of literacy and language teaching.
Special rates on a range of practical and useful publications on aspects of literacy teaching such as this.
The opportunity to attend meetings of local councils and annual conferences at which you can keep up to date with the latest ideas and research in literacy and language.

Individual membership costs £22 per year and School membership £27. For further details, write to UKRA, Unit 2, Station Road, Shepreth, Nr Royston, Herts. SG8 6PZ, United Kingdom

Teaching literacy requires professional knowledge. Membership of UKRA can help.